Step back in time with the PM dinosaurs as you learn Victorian Modern Cursive handwriting.

My name is

My teacher's name is

My learning goals and success criteria:

- I can trace and write all lower-case letters of the alphabet.
- I can trace and write all capital letters of the alphabet.
- I can trace and write all numerals 1 to 100.

Are you ready to write?

Posture

Is your back resting against the chair?

Are your feet flat on the floor?

Paper position

left-handed

Are you holding the paper steady with your non-writing hand?

right-handed

Pencil grip

Is one finger on top of the pencil?

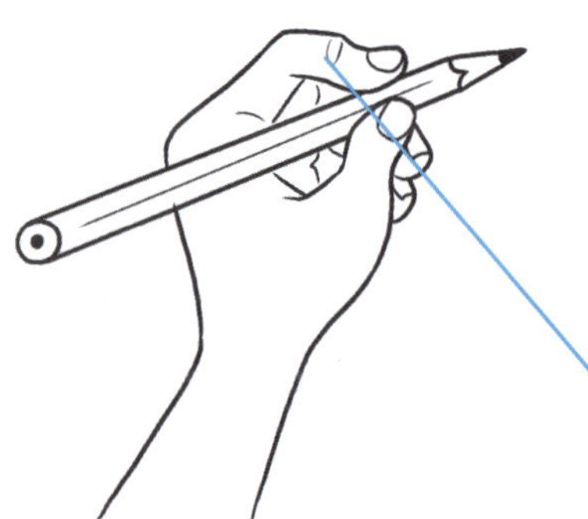

Left-handers, hold your pencil a little further up so you can see your handwriting!

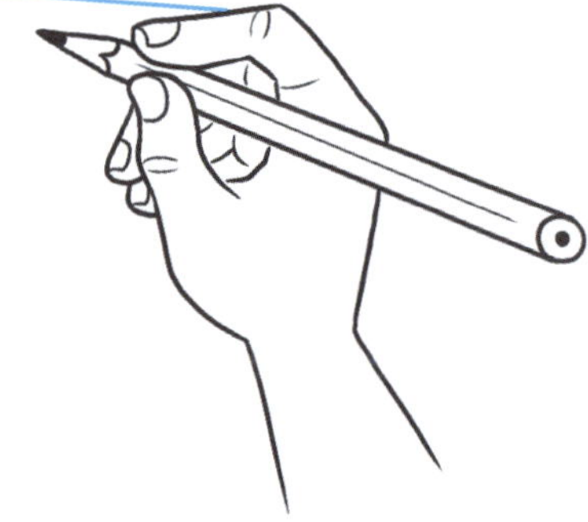

1, 2, 3, 4! Are my feet flat on the floor?
5, 6, 7, 8! Is my back up nice and straight?
9, 10, 11, 12! Show me how your pencil's held!
Thumb and pointer side-by-side, lucky tall one takes a ride!

Downstroke letter patterns

Try these downstroke patterns. Start at the dots. Follow the arrows.

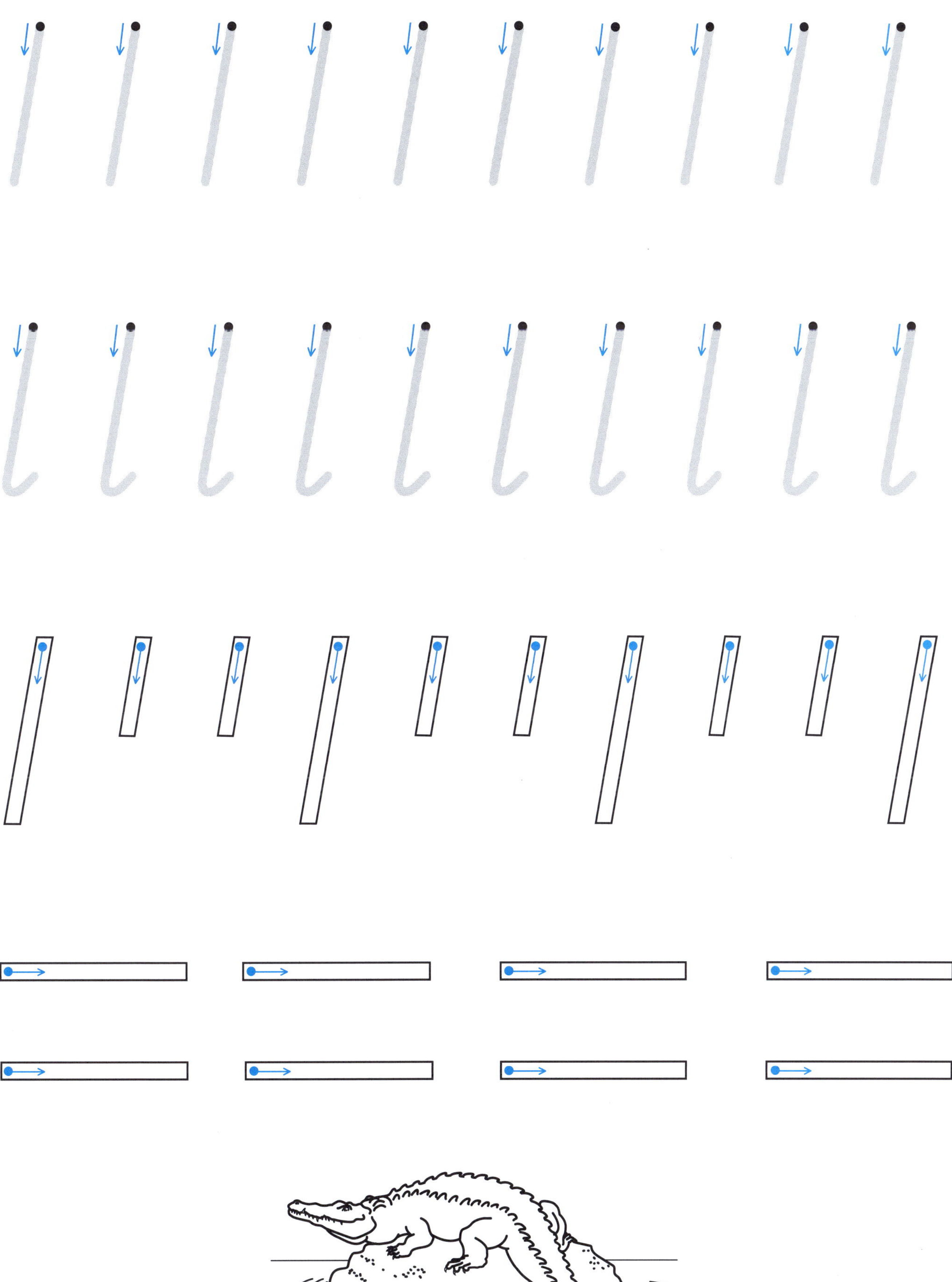

Downstroke letters

Trace.

Trace and copy.

Which letter have you traced or copied the most carefully?

Find your best lower-case *l* and place a tick neatly above it. Do the same for your best capital *L*.

Trace and copy.

Little Dinosaur saw the

lizard hiding in the leaves.

Trace the leaf shapes.

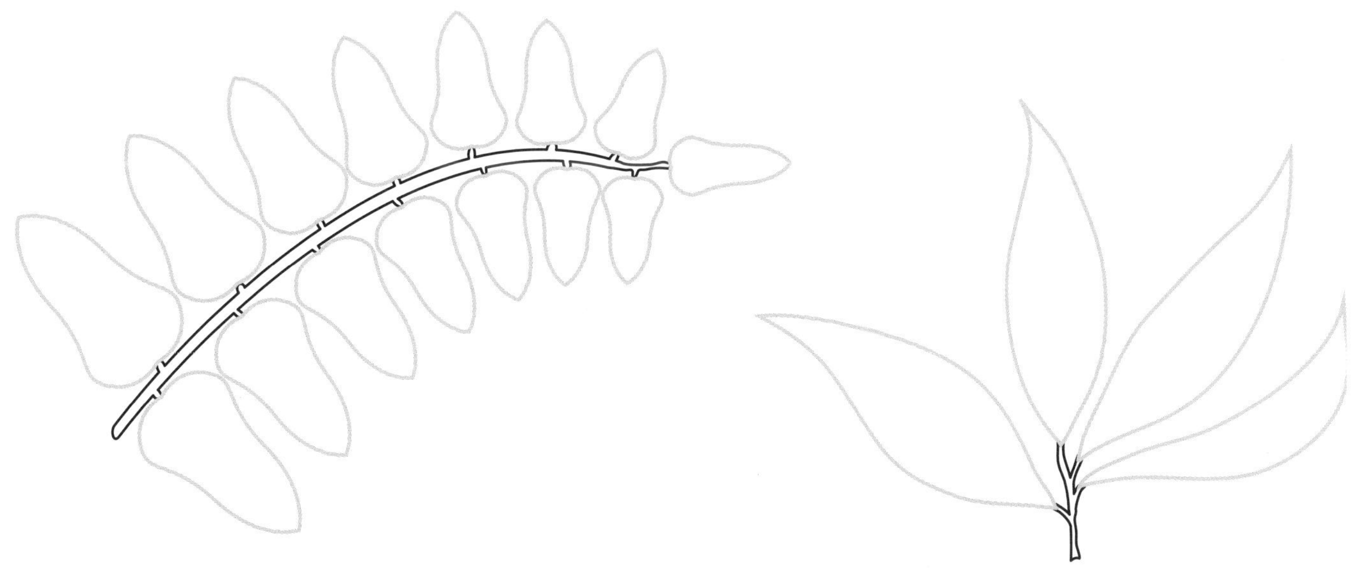

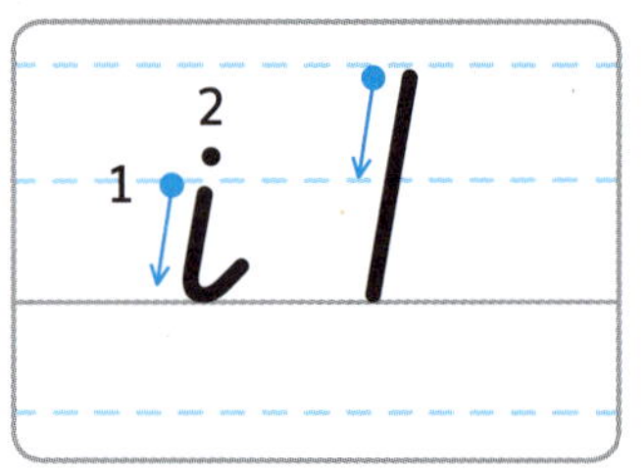

Trace.

Trace and copy.

in important inside its

insect invitation instinct

Find your best lower-case *i* and place a tick neatly above it. Do the same for your best capital *I*.

Trace and copy.

Little Dinosaur raced into

the cave, just in time.

The letter 'i' is a vowel. There are five vowels: a, e, i, o and u. Draw a neat circle around each vowel in the sentence above.

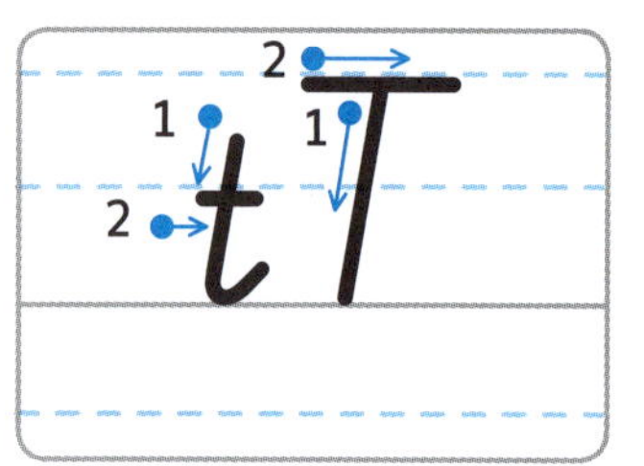

Trace.

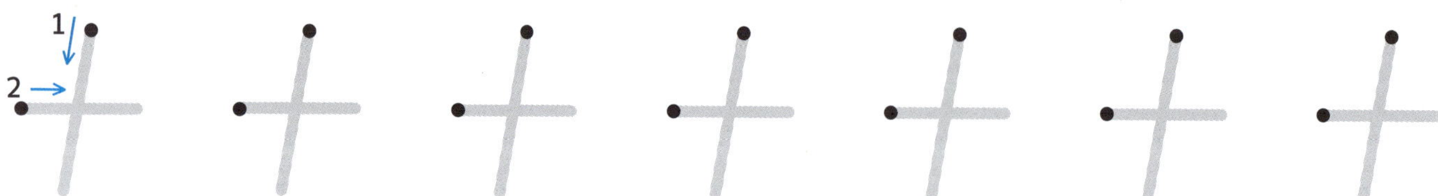

Trace and copy.

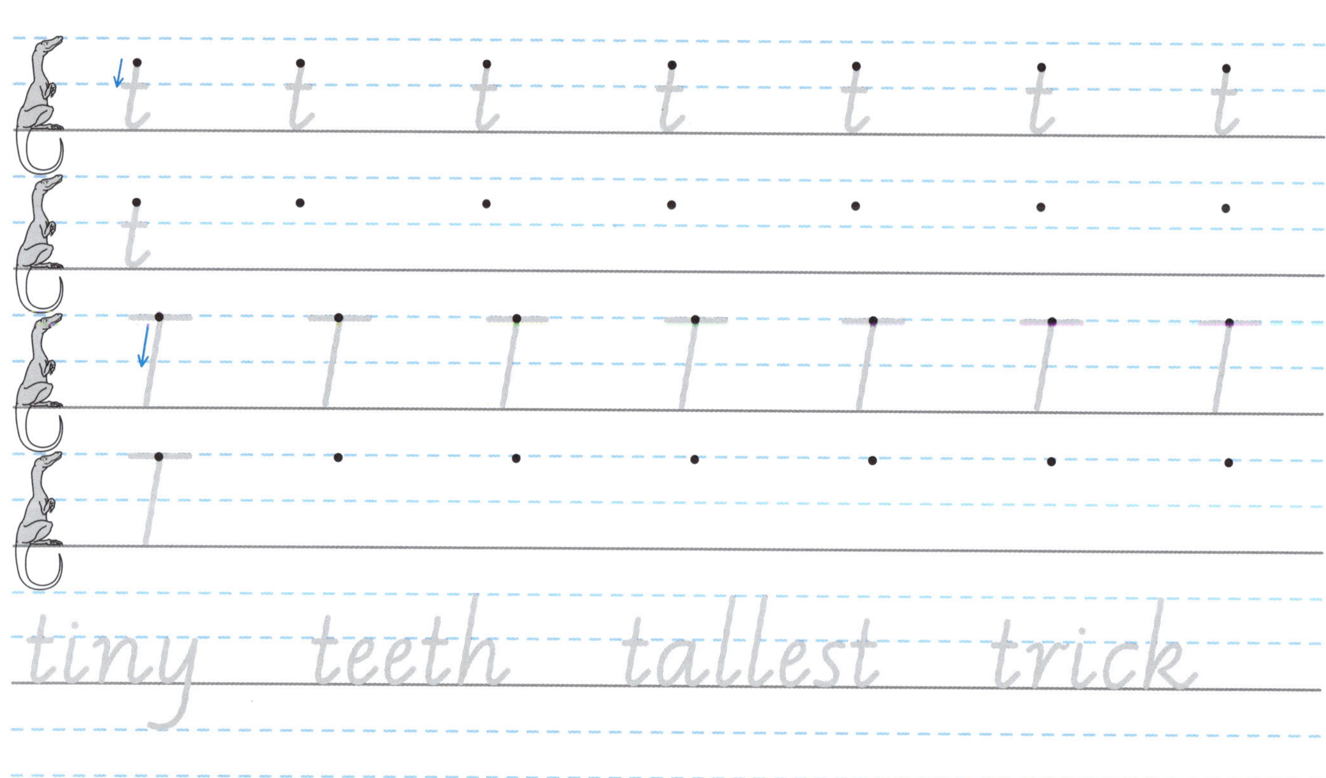

torch them tremble

Find your best lower-case *t* and place a tick neatly above it. Do the same for your best capital *T*.

Trace and copy.

big teeth, but brave

Triceratops did not tremble.

The letter *t* has a diagonal exit. Circle the diagonal exits.

t t t t t t t

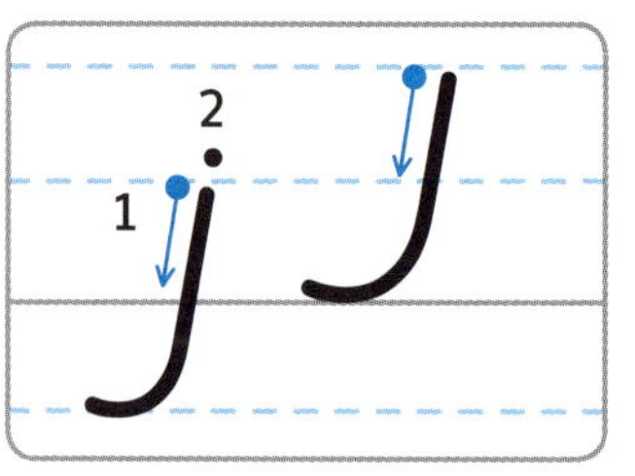

Trace.

J J J J J J J

Trace and copy.

j j j j j j j j

j

j j j j j j j j

j

jaw jumping journey

join joy just joke

Find your best lower-case j and place a tick neatly above it. Do the same for your best capital J.

Trace and copy.

enjoy jet jelly

banjo jump job

jars judge ninja

Can you neatly rewrite the words above in alphabetical order?

Hint: when the first letters are the same, use the second letter in each word to decide alphabetical order.

a b c d e f g h i j k l m n o p q r s t u v w x y z

Self-assessment: Downstroke letters

Trace and copy.

l L i I t T j J

Circle the downstroke letters in the word below.

triceratops

In the boxes below, write the downstroke letters in the order they appear in the alphabet. The starting dots will give you clues.

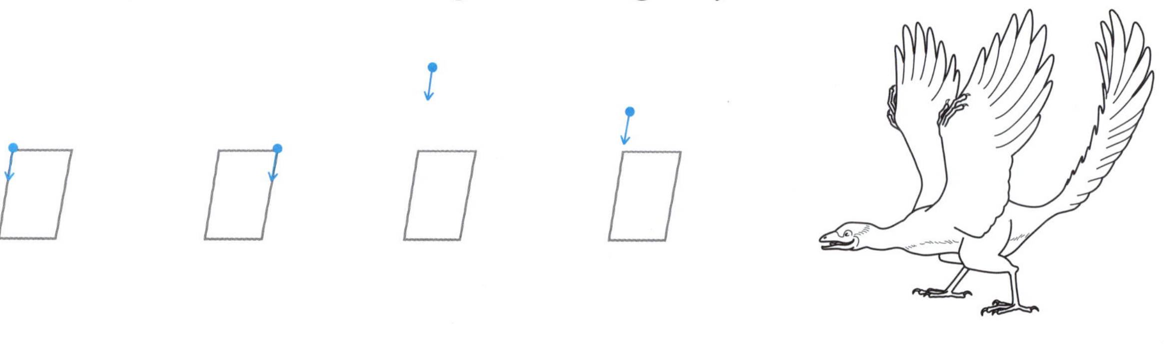

get.ga/PMWA150

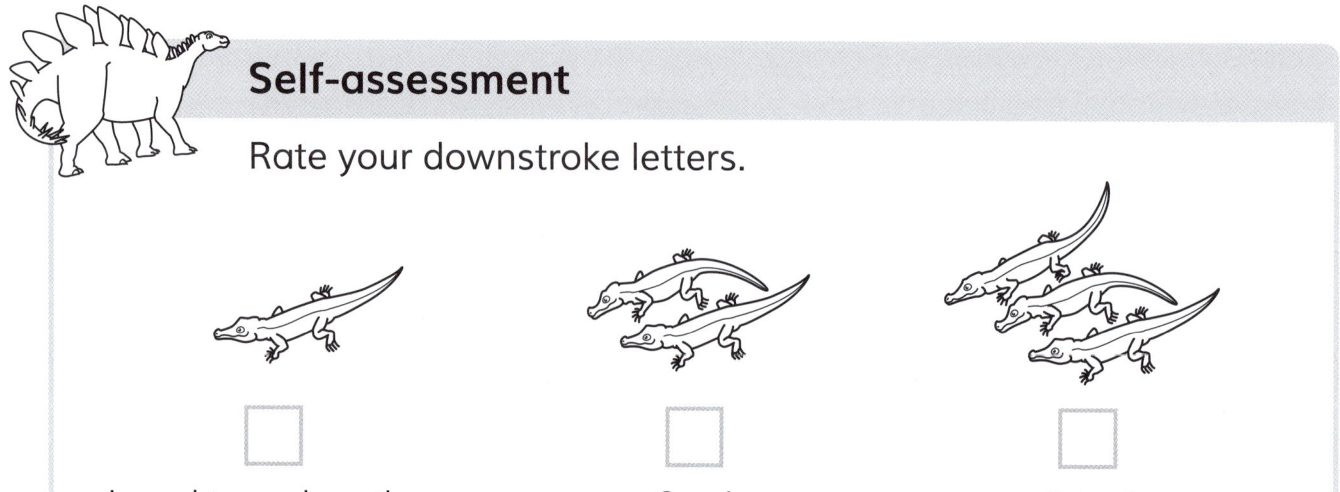

Self-assessment

Rate your downstroke letters.

I need to work on these.

Good.

Great!

Closed anti-clockwise letter patterns

Try these anti-clockwise patterns. Start at the dots. Follow the arrows.

Closed anti-clockwise letters

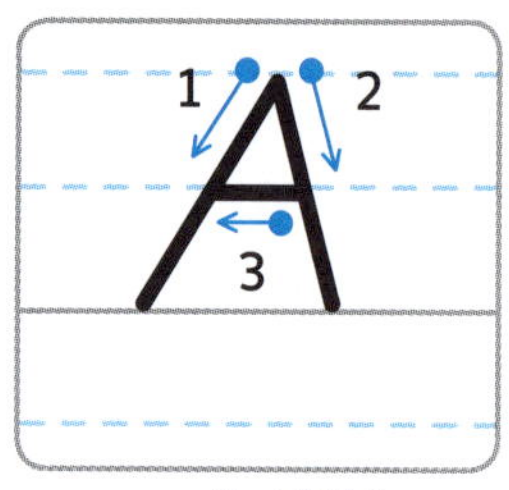

capital 'A' for left-handers

Trace.

ele ele ele ele ele

Trace and copy.

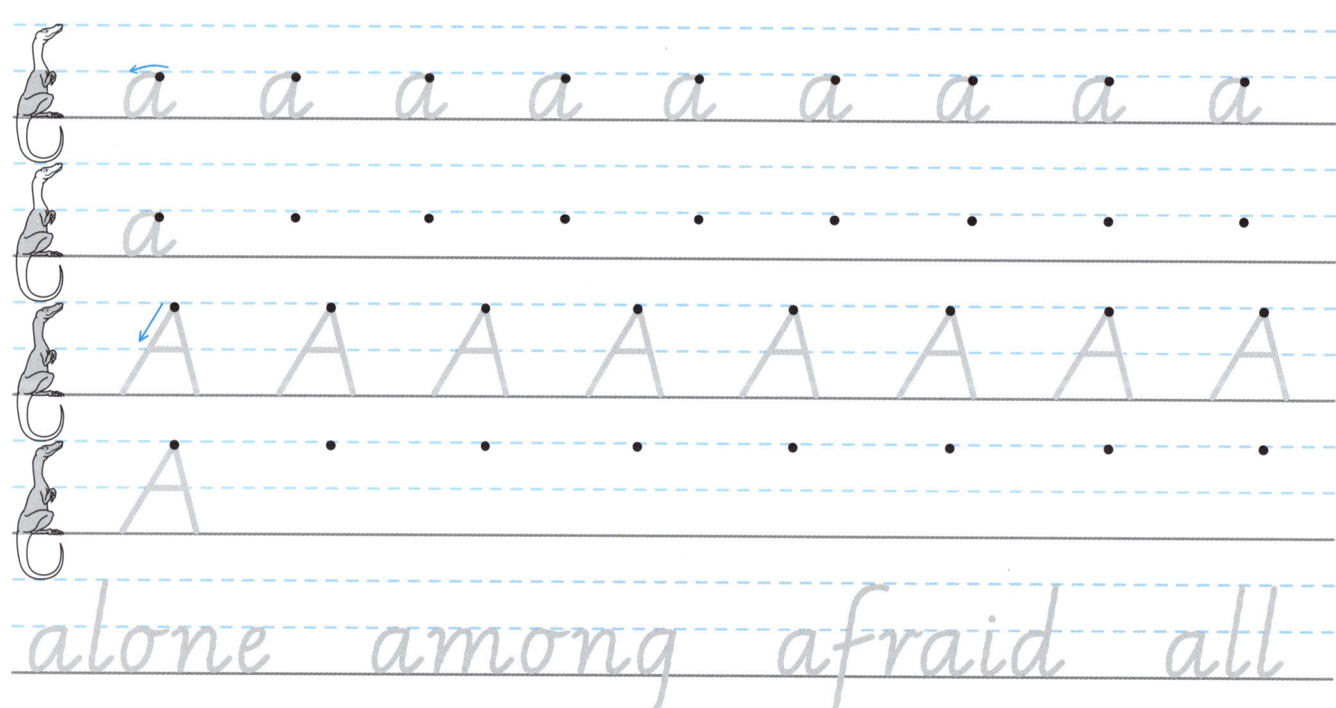

Which letter have you traced or copied the most carefully?

Find your best lower-case *a* and place a tick neatly above it. Do the same for your best capital *A*.

Trace and copy.

Little Dinosaur was not

afraid. He knew he was not

alone. He was among friends.

Spelling tip

Do you want an easy way to remember how to spell the word 'friend'?

'I have a fri<u>end</u> until the <u>end</u>!'

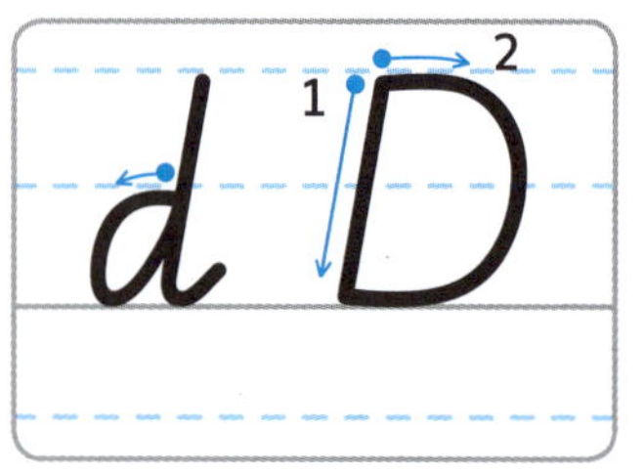

Trace.

Trace and copy.

d d d d d d d d

d

D D D D D D D D

D

deep dinosaur disappear

down danger middle

Find your best lower-case d and place a tick neatly above it. Do the same for your best capital D.

Trace and copy.

Small Duck-bill looked

for the other duck-bills.

Had they disappeared?

Punctuation practice

A question mark goes at the end of a question.

Find the question mark in the text above. Circle it neatly.
Trace and copy some question marks of your own.

? ? ? ? ? ? ? ?

ISBN: 9780170424042

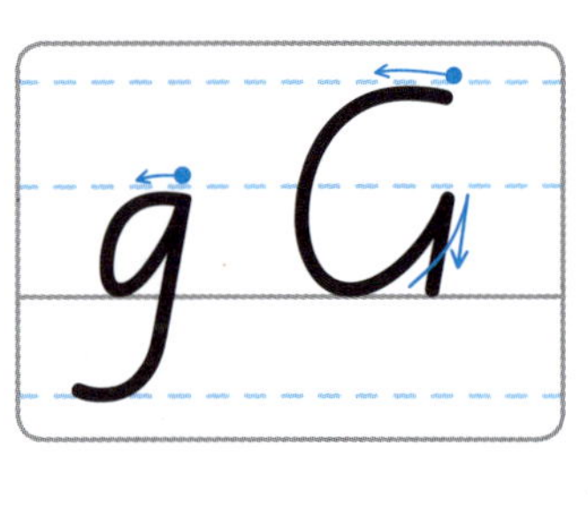

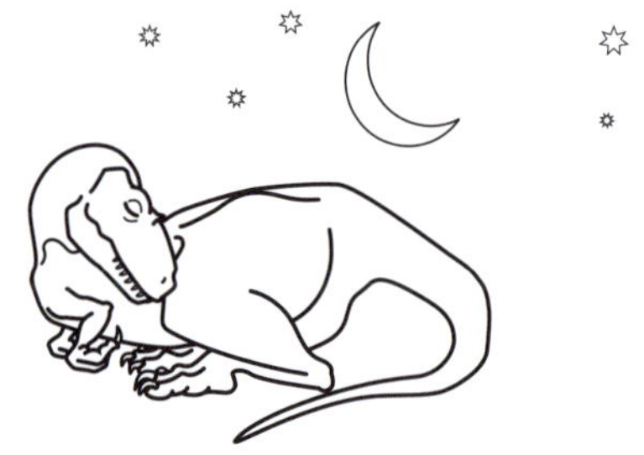

Trace.

Trace and copy.

g g g g g g g g

g

G G G G G G G G

G

grown goodnight Gorgo

got green going long

Find your best lower-case g and place a tick neatly above it. Do the same for your best capital G.

Trace and copy.

Gorgo was big and strong.

Now she was fully grown,

she was nine metres long!

get.ga/PMWA151

Punctuation practice

An exclamation mark goes at the end of a sentence to add emphasis or show strong feelings.

Find the exclamation mark in the text above. Circle it neatly.
Trace and copy some exclamation marks of your own.

! ! ! ! ! ! ! !

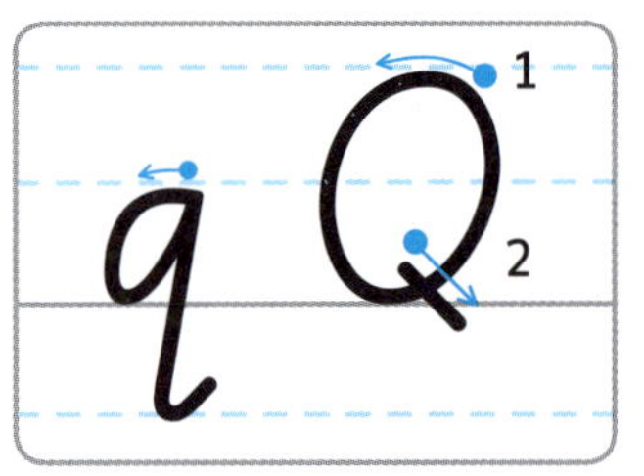

Trace.

l l l l l l l l

Trace and copy.

quietly question quickly

quiz equal squid quite

Find your best lower-case q and place a tick neatly above it. Do the same for your best capital Q.

Trace and copy, then complete the answer.

Q: Do you know which

Q:

animals are the closest

living relatives to dinosaurs?

A: b _ r _ s

A:

Can you write a dinosaur question of your own?

Find your best lower-case σ and place a tick neatly above it. Do the same for your best capital O.

Trace and copy the poem. Create your own ending on a new sheet of paper.

Dinosaur, dinosaur,

Turn around.

Dinosaur, dinosaur,

Stomp the ground!

ISBN: 9780170424042

Self-assessment: Closed anti-clockwise letters

Trace and copy.

aA dD gG qQ oO

aA dD gG qQ oO

Circle the closed anti-clockwise letters in the word below.

dinosaur

get.ga/PMWA152

Self-assessment

Rate your closed anti-clockwise letters.

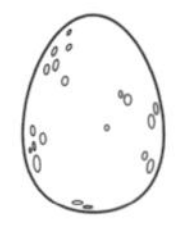

I need to work on these.

Good.

Great!

ISBN: 9780170424042

Open anti-clockwise letter patterns

Try these anti-clockwise patterns. Start at the dots. Follow the arrows.

ISBN: 9780170424042

Open anti-clockwise letters

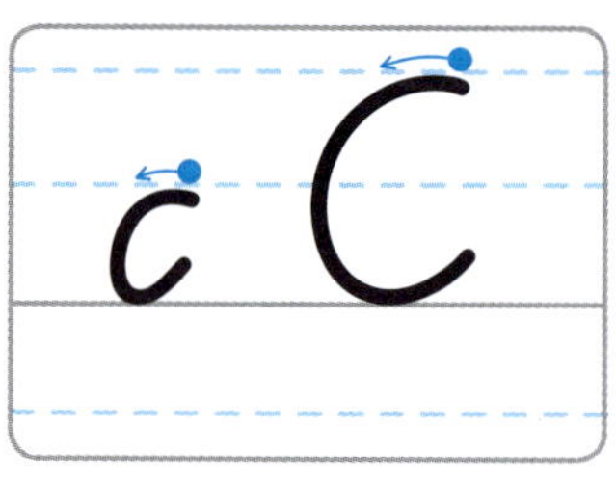

Trace.

Trace and copy.

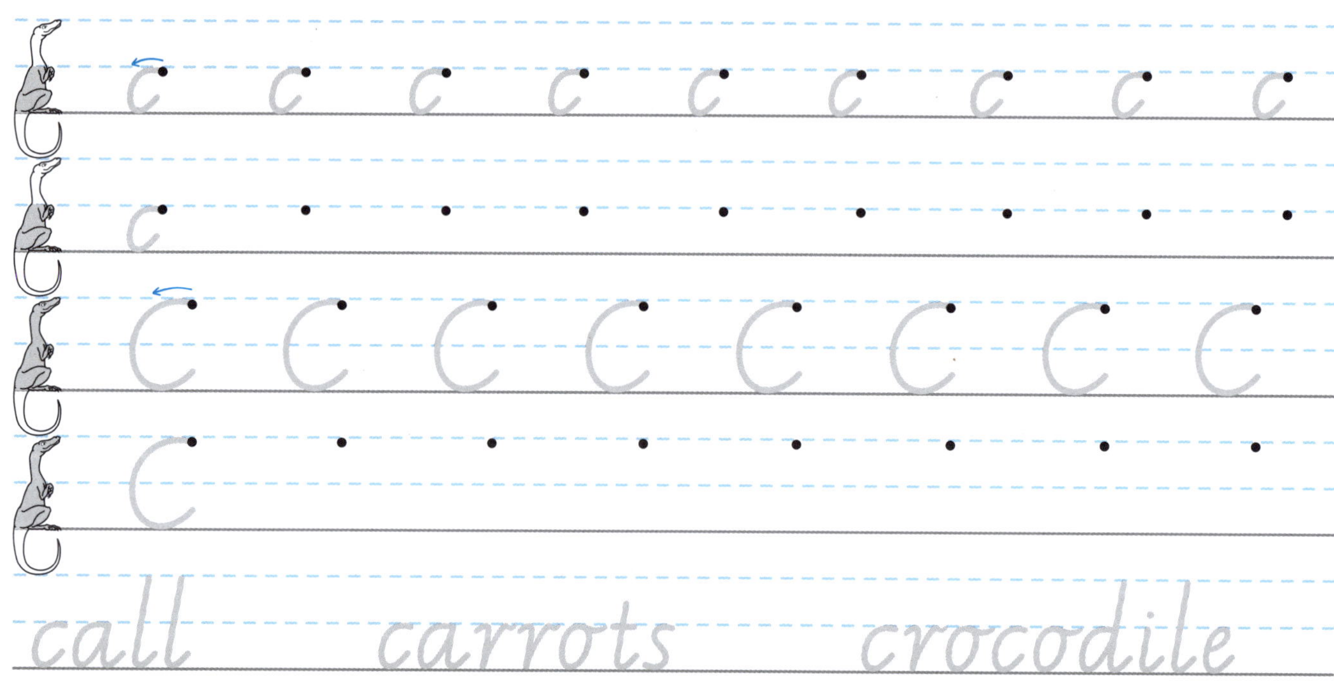

Which letter have you traced or copied the most carefully?

Find your best lower-case *c* and place a tick neatly above it. Do the same for your best capital *C*.

ISBN: 9780170424042

Trace and copy.

Q: What do you call a

Q:

stegosaurus with carrots

in its ears?

A: You can call it

A:

anything you like.

It can't hear you!

I hope you like dinosaur jokes!

ISBN: 9780170424042

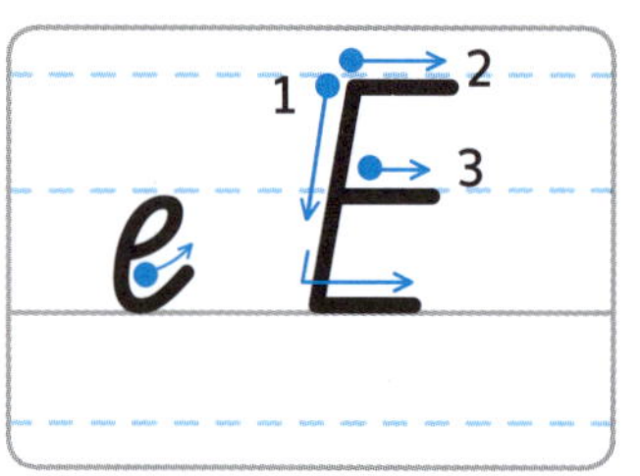

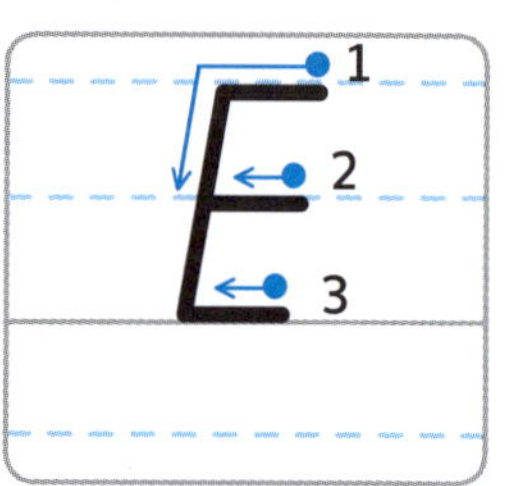

capital 'E' for left-handers

Trace.

eee eee eee eee eee

Trace and copy.

e e e e e e e e e

e

E E E E E E E E

E

eggs empty eaten each

eyes elephant every

Find your best lower-case *e* and place a tick neatly above it. Do the same for your best capital *E*.

Trace and copy.

Q: How many dinosaurs

Q:

can fit in an empty box?

A: One. After that, the

A:

box isn't empty any more!

Draw your favourite dinosaur inside the box.

ISBN: 9780170424042

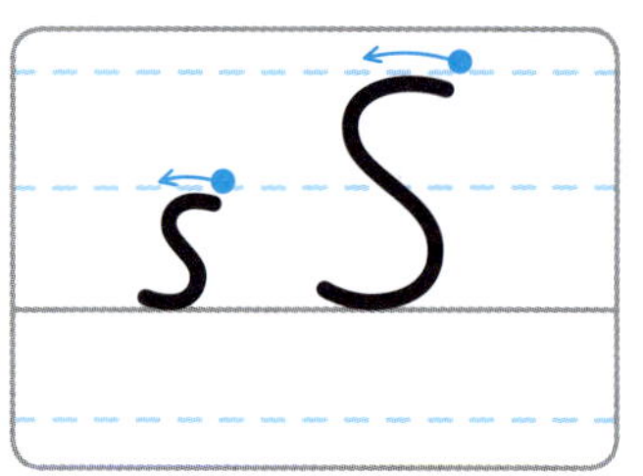

Trace.

Trace and copy.

s s s s s s s s

s

S S S S S S S S

S

smell shake splashes she

six sound stop fossil

Find your best lower-case *s* and place a tick neatly above it. Do the same for your best capital *S*.

ISBN: 9780170424042

Trace and copy.

Q: What do you call a

Q:

fossil that doesn't ever

want to work?

A: Lazy bones!

A:

Punctuation practice

You can use an apostrophe to show where letters have been left out of a contraction.

Trace the following contractions. Draw neat circles around the apostrophes.

you're can't he's won't

ISBN: 9780170424042

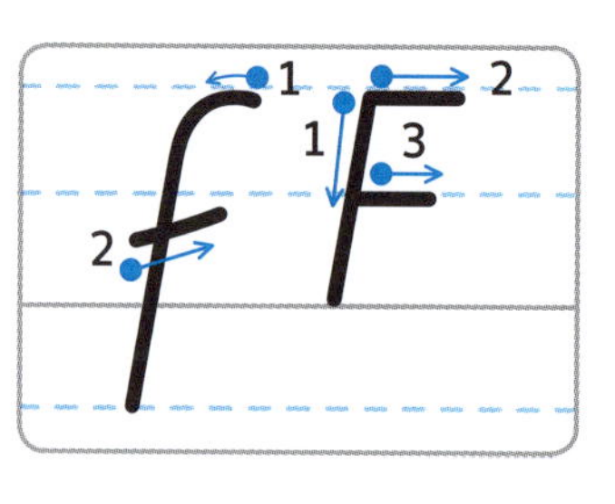

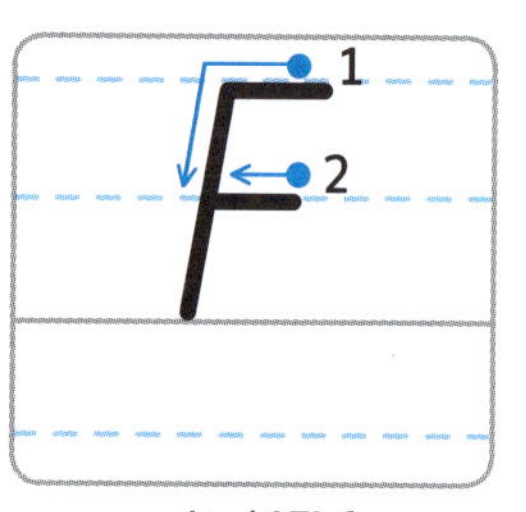

capital 'F' for left-handers

Trace.

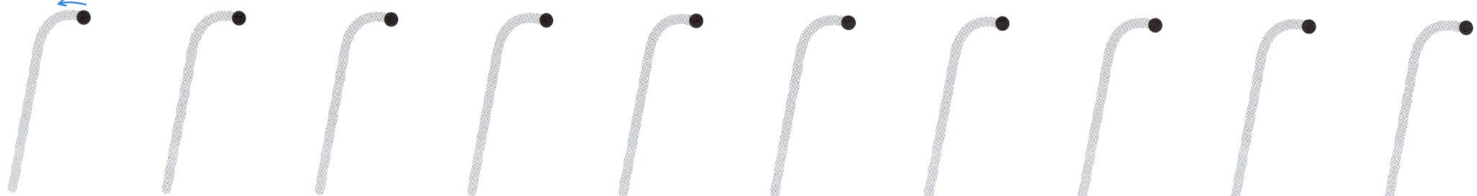

Trace and copy.

f

F

fern forest find finish

far fear flight cliff

Find your best lower-case f and place a tick neatly above it. Do the same for your best capital F.

ISBN: 9780170424042

Trace and copy.

The triceratops had to go

far away from the forest

to forage for food.

Draw a neat circle around every letter *f* in the sentence above.

Trace and complete the sentence.

The letter f is a head,

body and t_______ letter.

ISBN: 9780170424042

Trace.

uu uu uu uu

Trace and copy.

u u u u u u u

u

U U U U U U U

U

up underneath unroll use

untied understand until

Find your best lower-case *u* and place a tick neatly above it. Do the same for your best capital *U*.

ISBN: 9780170424042

Trace and copy.

Q: What do you call

Q:

a clever dinosaur that

never gives up?

A: 

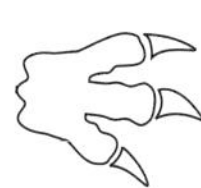

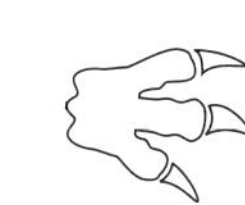

get.ga/PMWA153

ISBN: 9780170424042

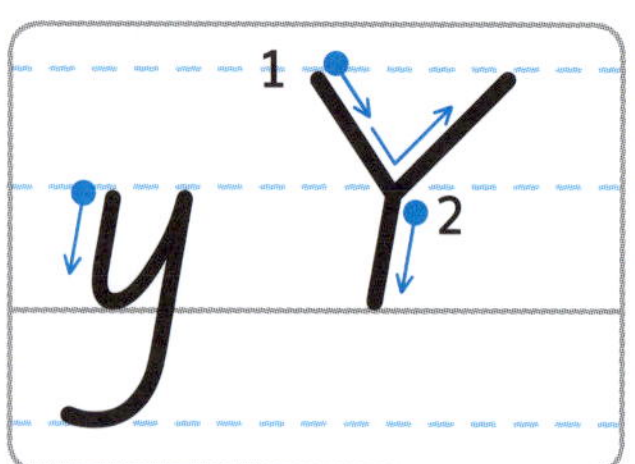

Trace.

Trace and copy.

y y y y y y y y

y

Y Y Y Y Y Y Y Y

Y

year young yesterday

yes yellow yawn you're

Find your best lower-case y and place a tick neatly above it. Do the same for your best capital Y.

ISBN: 9780170424042

Trace and copy.

dinosaur came out of his

hole. Little Dinosaur was

looking for adventure.

ISBN: 9780170424042

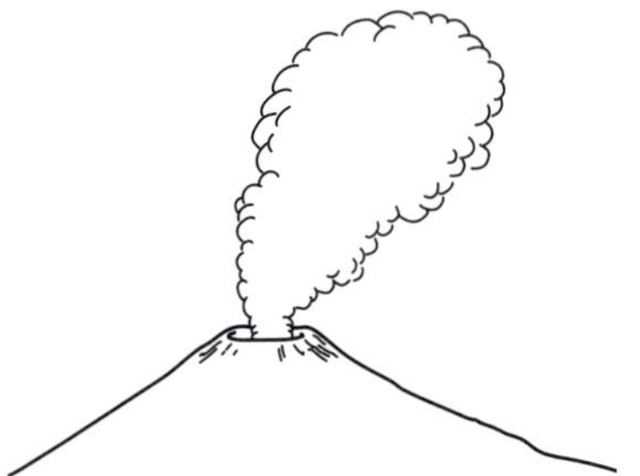

Trace.

ιιι ιιι ιιι ιιι ιιι

Trace and copy.

v v v v v v v v

v

V V V V V V V V

V

volcano village lava very

valley arrive over above

Find your best lower-case v and place a tick neatly above it. Do the same for your best capital V.

ISBN: 9780170424042

Trace and copy.

Rivers of hot, red lava

came down the sides of

the volcano into the valley.

ISBN: 9780170424042

w W

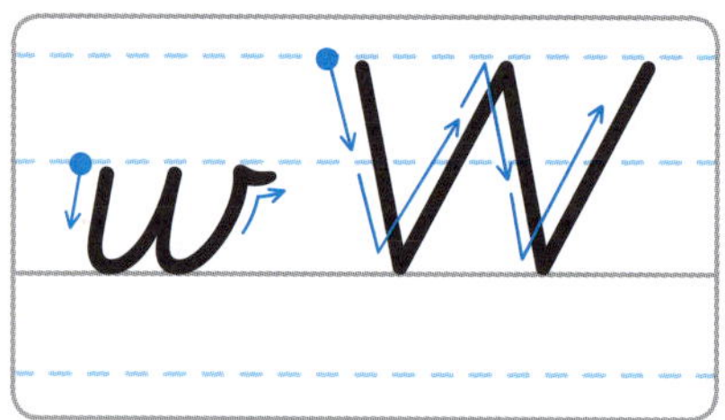

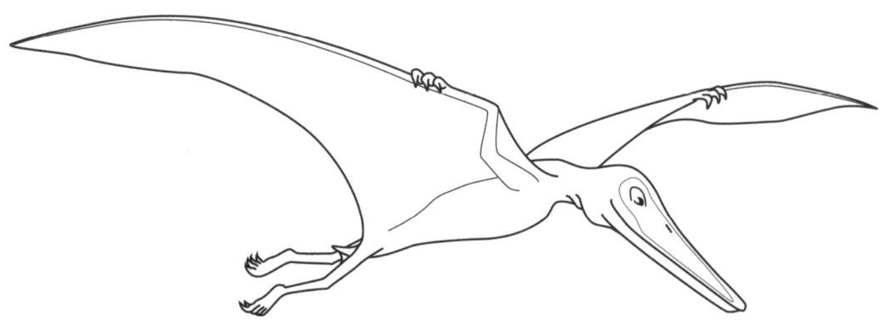

Trace.

Trace and copy.

w w w w w w w w

w

W W W W W W W

W

was what wingspan

would weather wide

Find your best lower-case *w* and place a tick neatly above it. Do the same for your best capital *W*.

ISBN: 9780170424042

Trace and copy.

Q: What was the

Q:

wingspan of a pterosaur?

Complete the sum, then trace and copy.

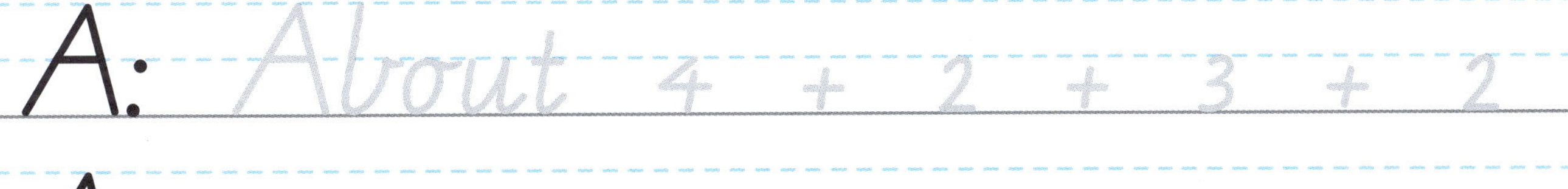
A: About 4 + 2 + 3 + 2

A:

= ________ metres long.

get.ga/PMWA154

Colour the wedge in each letter *w* below.

w w w w w w

ISBN: 9780170424042

Trace.

uuu uuu uuu

Trace and copy.

b b b b b b b b

b

B B B B B B B B

B

baby broke born be

before best nibbled

Find your best lower-case b and place a tick neatly above it. Do the same for your best capital B.

Trace and copy.

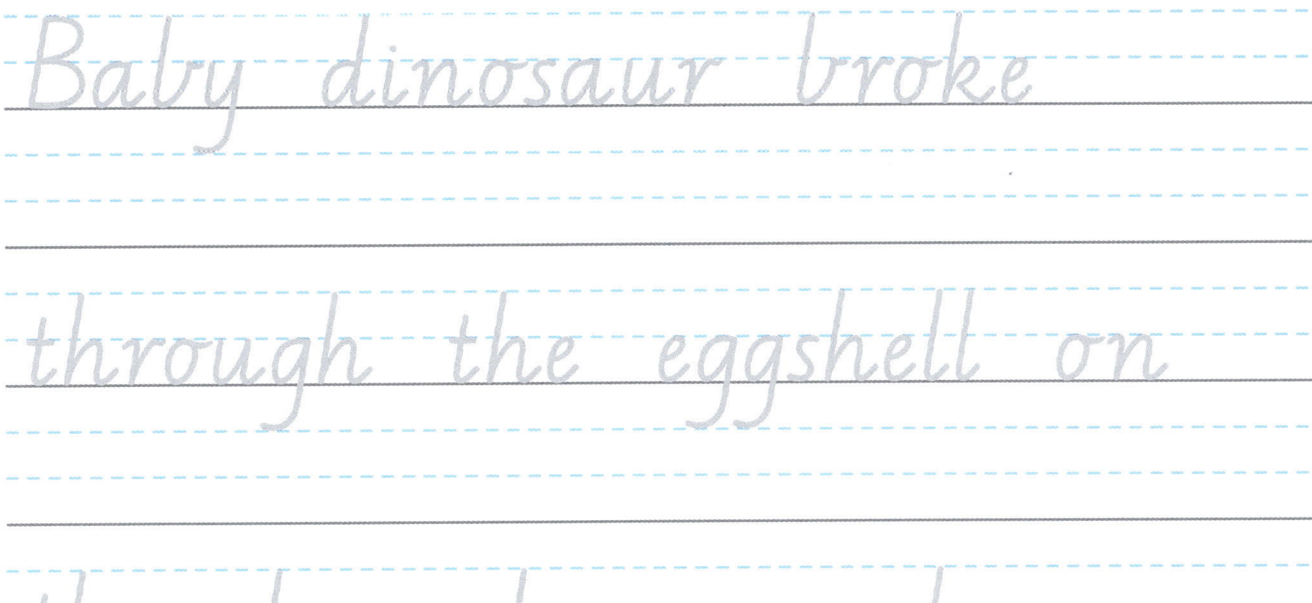

The letter b has a horizontal exit. Circle the horizontal exits.

b b b b b b

ISBN: 9780170424042

Self-assessment: Open anti-clockwise letters

Trace and copy.

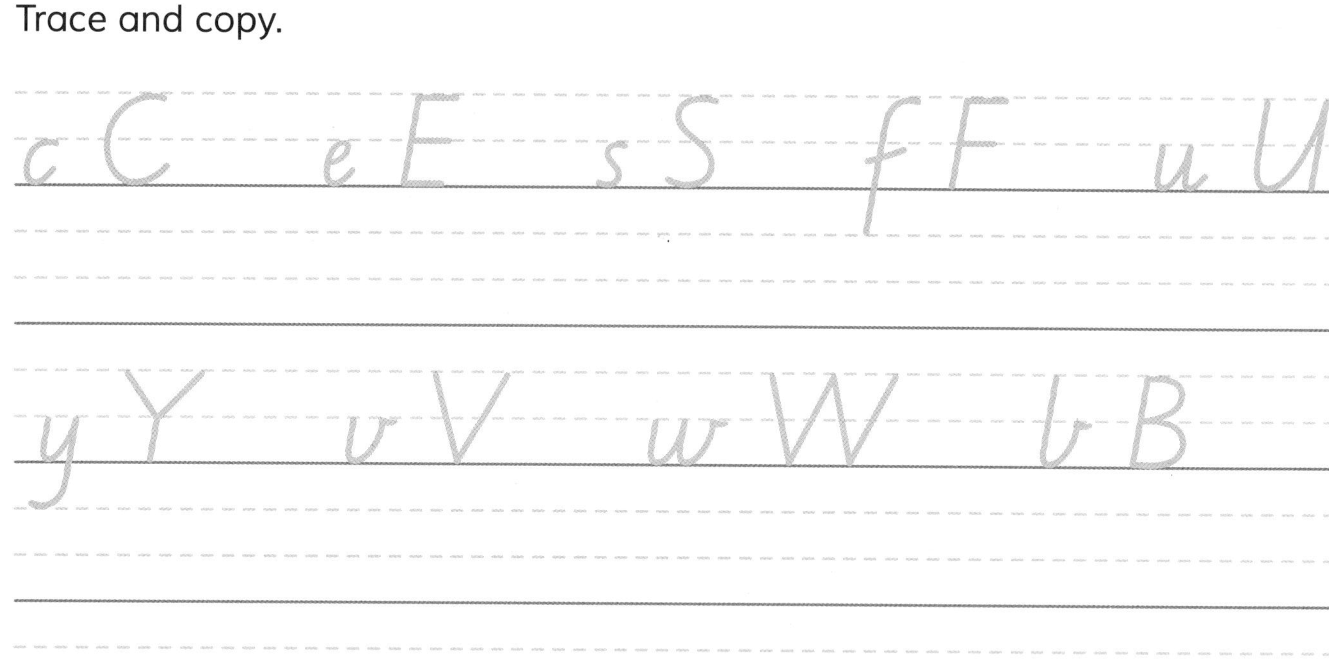

Circle the open anti-clockwise letters in the word below. Then colour all the wedges.

stegosaurus

get.ga/PMWA155

Self-assessment

Rate your open anti-clockwise letters.

☐ I need to work on these.

☐ Good.

☐ Great!

ISBN: 9780170424042

Clockwise letter patterns

Try these clockwise patterns. Start at the dots. Follow the arrows.

ISBN: 9780170424042

Clockwise letters

Trace.

Trace and copy.

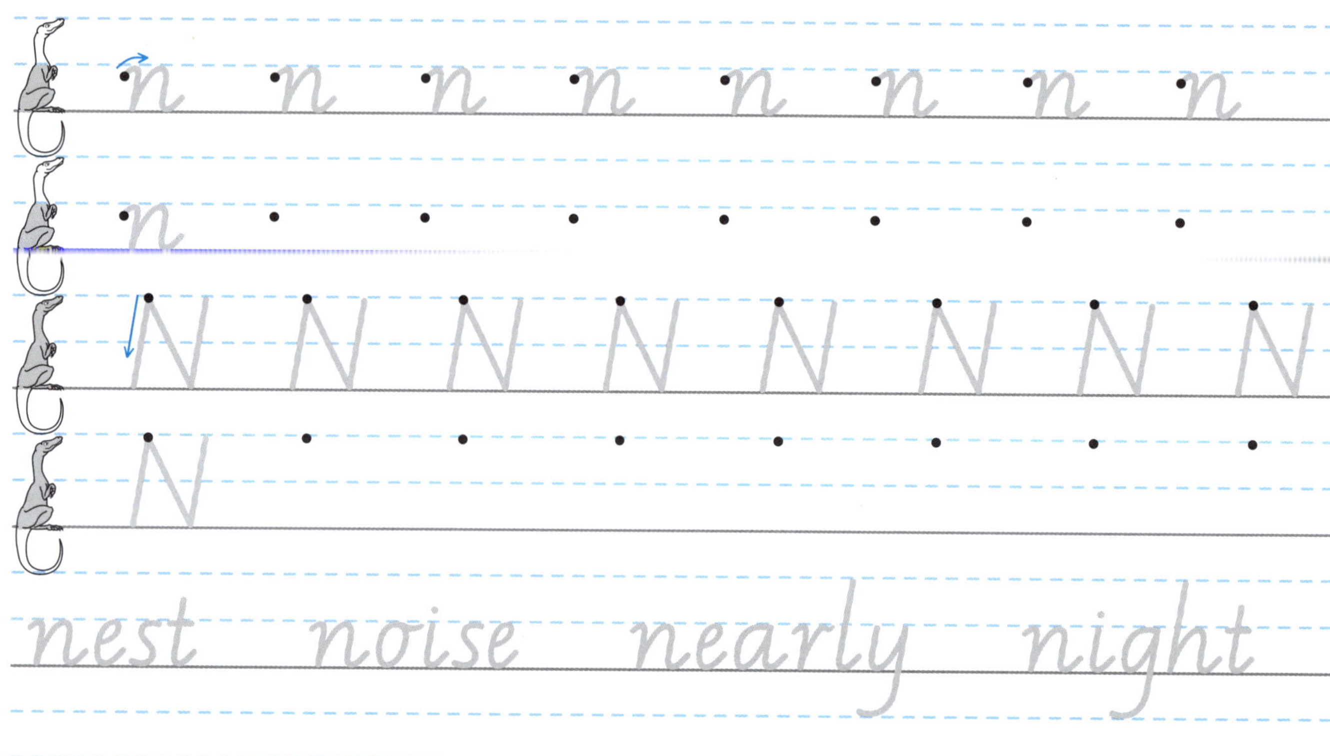

Which letter have you traced or copied the most carefully?

Find your best lower-case *n* and place a tick neatly above it. Do the same for your best capital *N*.

ISBN: 9780170424042

Trace and copy.

"Tyrannosaurus Rex is

nearly here! Don't make a

noise." The baby dinosaurs

ran to hide in their nest.

Colour the wedge in each letter *n* below.

n n n n n n n

Trace.

m m m m

Trace and copy.

m m m m m m m

m

M M M M M M M

M

mighty move meat-eater

middle most morning

Find your best lower-case *m* and place a tick neatly above it. Do the same for your best capital *M*.

Trace and copy.

The mighty, hungry

meat-eater was moving

through the massive trees.

The letter *m* has a rounded entry and a diagonal exit. Circle the rounded entries and diagonal exits.

m m m m m

ISBN: 9780170424042

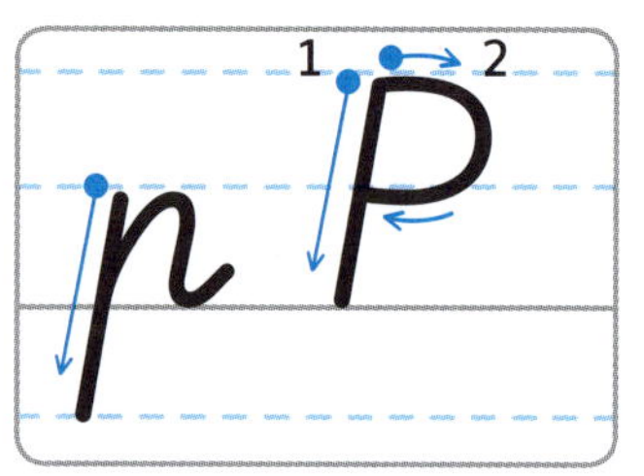

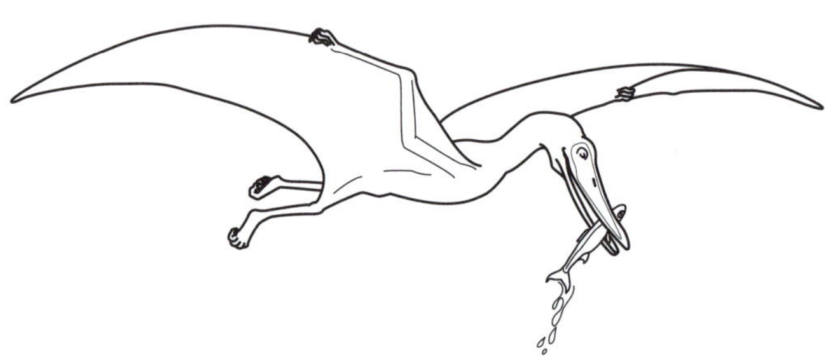

Trace.

r r r r r r r r

Trace and copy.

p p p p p p p p

p

P P P P P P P P

P

plant prey people past

power parents predator

Find your best lower-case p and place a tick neatly above it. Do the same for your best capital P.

Trace and copy.

Before there were any people,

there were dinosaurs. Some,

like allosaurus, chased their

prey. Others, like diplodocus,

were plant-eaters.

get.ga/PMWA156

ISBN: 9780170424042

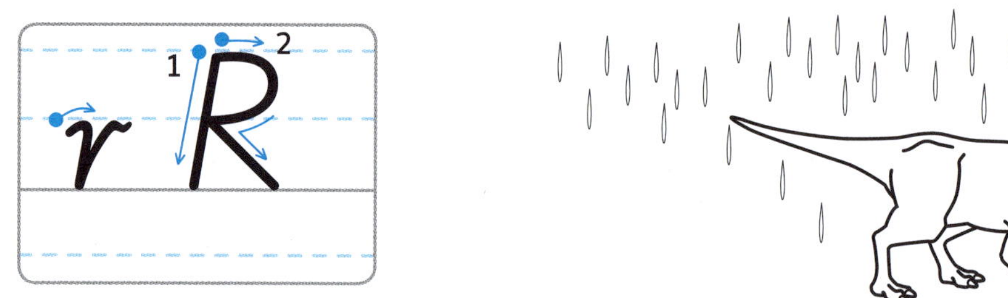

Trace.

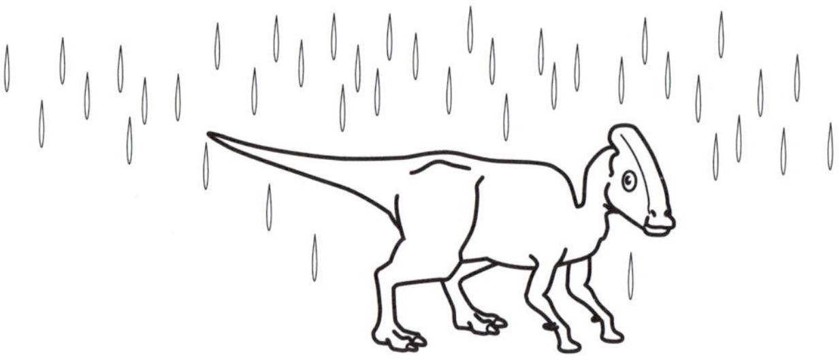

Trace and copy.

r r r r r r r r

r

R R R R R R R R

R

rain river raptor run

rumble roared hurry

Find your best lower-case *r* and place a tick neatly above it. Do the same for your best capital *R*.

Trace and copy.

to cross the river before the

rain poured down.

The letter *r* has a rounded entry. Circle the rounded entries.

r r r r r r r

ISBN: 9780170424042

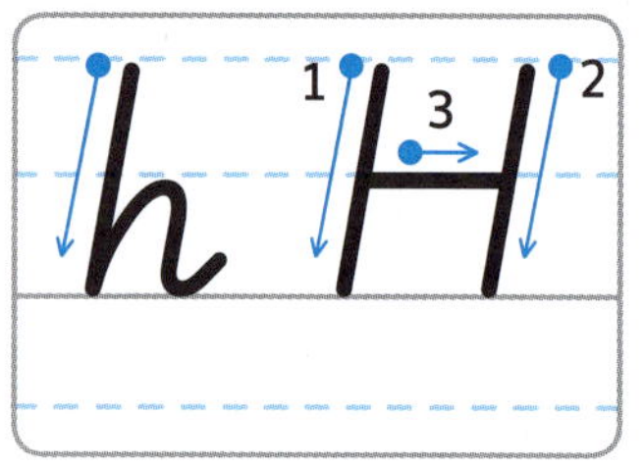

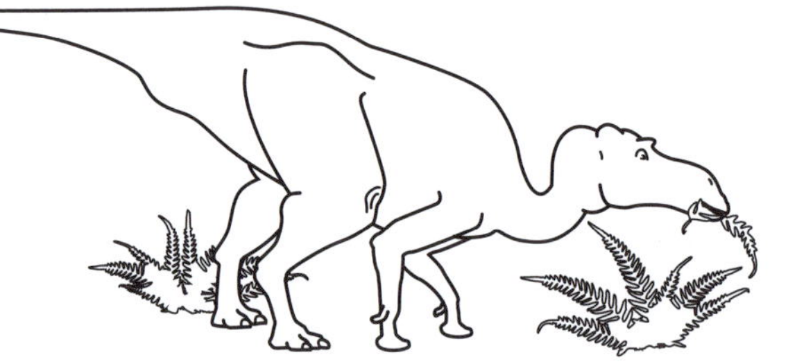

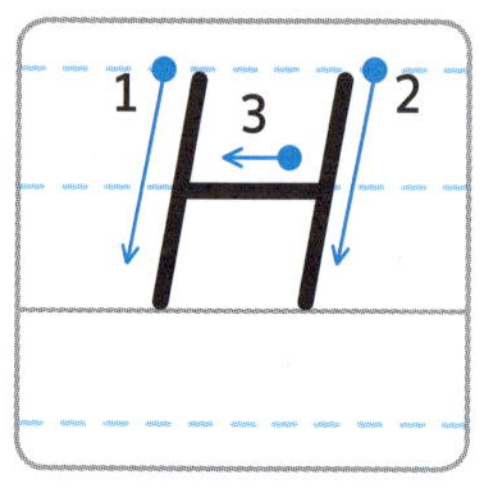

capital 'H' for left-handers

Trace.

h h h h h

Trace and copy.

h h h h h h h h

h

H H H H H H H H

H

huge happy herbivore

hatch hungry heavy

Find your best lower-case *h* and place a tick neatly above it. Do the same for your best capital *H*.

Trace and copy.

The baby herbivore
hatched from his egg.
His huge father was
very happy to see him.

Circle the letters with wedges in the text above. Colour the wedges.

Trace.

Trace and copy.

k k k k k k k

k

K K K K K K K K

K

kick knocked knee

keep knew walk kind

Find your best lower-case k and place a tick neatly above it. Do the same for your best capital K.

Trace and copy.

The apatosauruses kicked

their legs, swimming until

they knew they were safely

across the deep, dark lake.

get.ga/PMWA157

Spelling tip

The letter 'k' is sometimes silent.

Draw a circle around the word with a silent *k* in the sentence above.

Some other words with silent *k*: *knee*, *knock*, *knit*, *knot*.

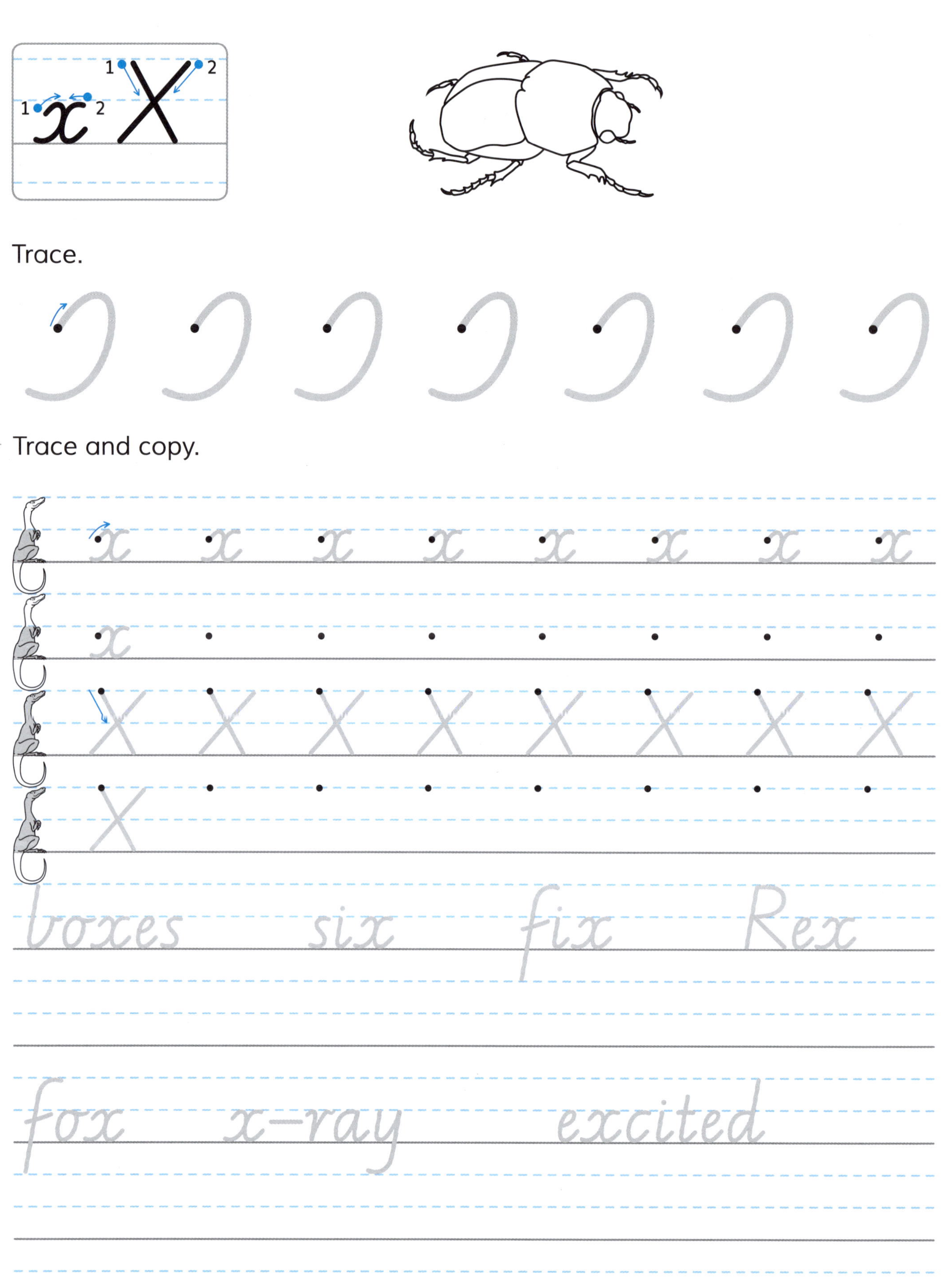

Find your best lower-case *x* and place a tick neatly above it. Do the same for your best capital X.

Trace and copy.

"Go away, Tyrannosaurus Rex,

so we can fix our nest!" said

the six baby dinosaurs.

Punctuation practice

Speech marks, or quotation marks, are used to show when someone is speaking. They always come in pairs.

Draw neat circles around the speech marks on this page.

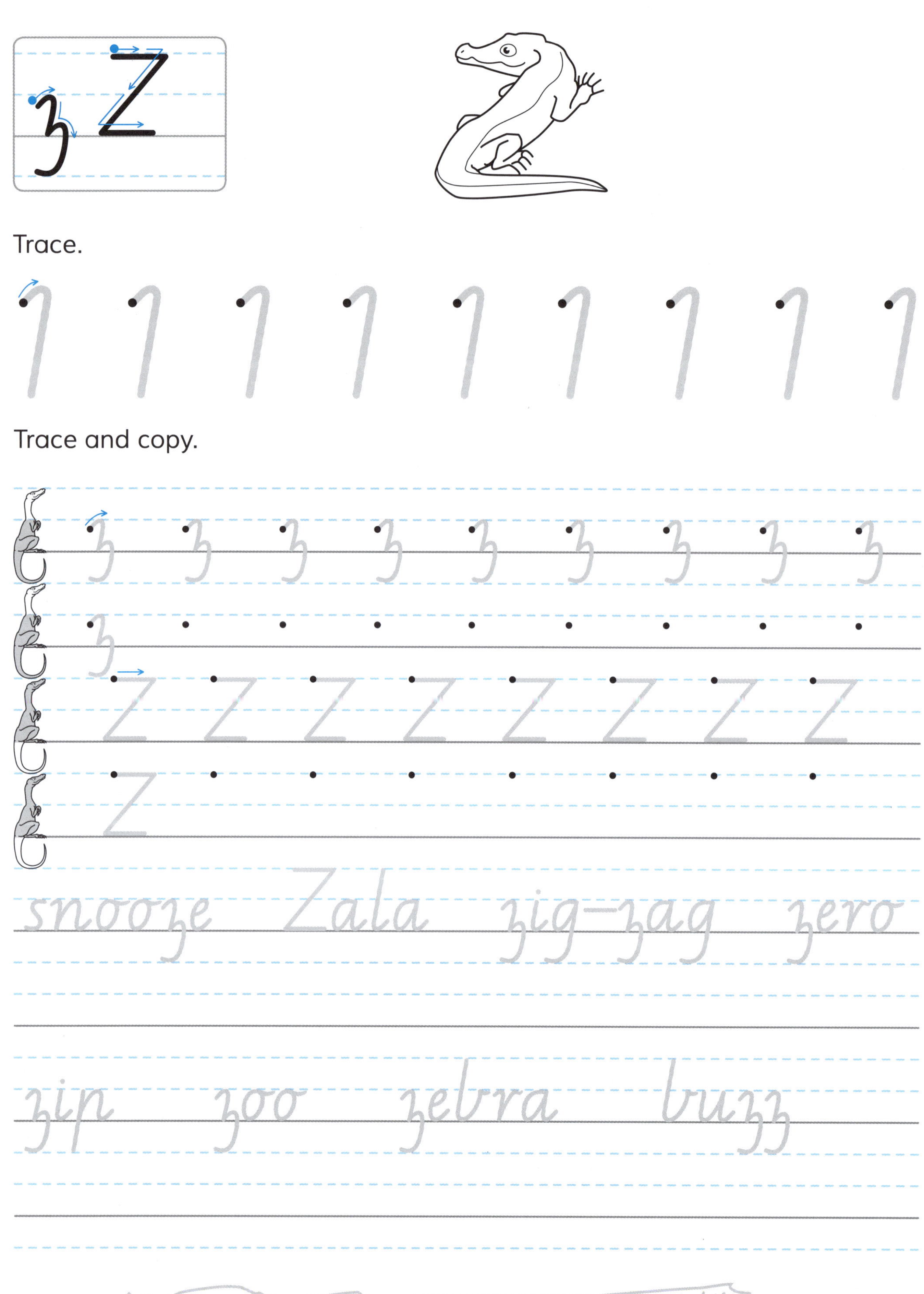

Find your best lower-case z and place a tick neatly above it. Do the same for your best capital Z.

Trace and copy.

Trace the sums and fill in the missing numbers. Then copy.

Self-assessment: Clockwise letters

Trace and copy.

n N   m M   p P   r R

h H   k K   x X   z Z

Circle the clockwise letters with rounded entries in the word below.

Tyrannosaurus

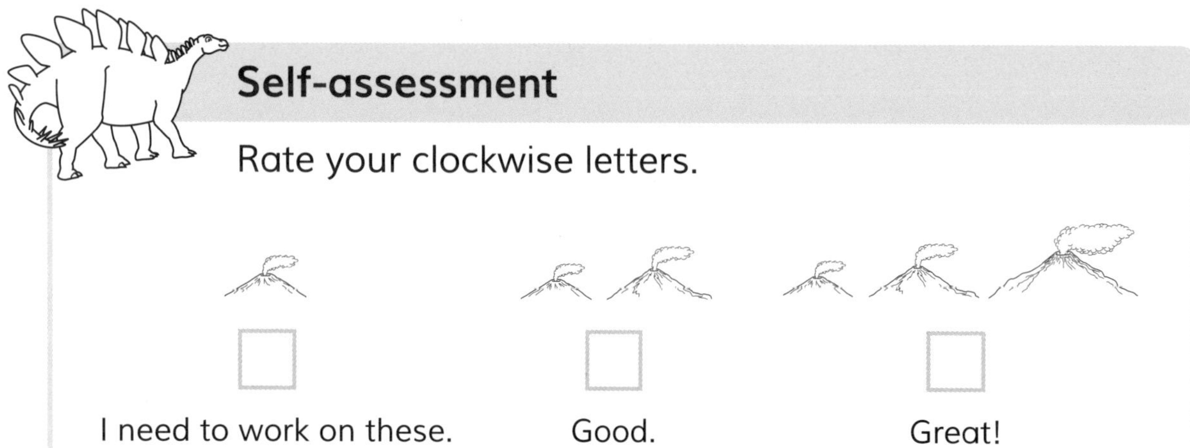

Self-assessment

Rate your clockwise letters.

☐ I need to work on these.

☐ Good.

☐ Great!

get.ga/PMWA158

Numerals

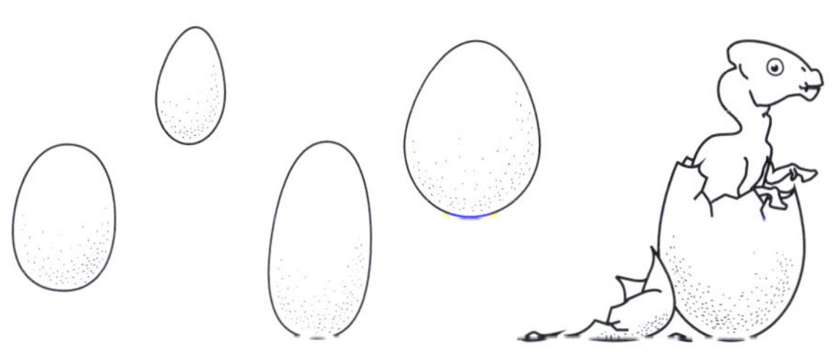

Trace and copy.

1 2 3 4 5 6 7 8 9 10

Trace and copy the numbers.

10 ten 20 twenty

30 thirty 40 forty

50 fifty 60 sixty

70 seventy 80 eighty

Teacher observation guide

Student is: left handed ☐ right handed ☐

Student demonstrates correct posture, paper position and pencil grip. ☐

Student is stroking from top to bottom. ☐

Student is stroking from left to right. ☐

Student is tracking and tracing patterns correctly using starting dots and arrows. ☐

Student is tracing letters correctly using starting dots and arrows. ☐

Student forms lower-case letters of a consistent size with accuracy:

a	b	c	d	e	f	g	h	i	j	k	l	m	n	o	p	q	r	s	t	u	v	w	x	y	z

Student forms capital letters of a consistent size with accuracy:

A	B	C	D	E	F	G	H	I	J	K	L	M	N	O	P	Q	R	S	T	U	V	W	X	Y	Z

Student uses head, body and tail character to describe the spatial properties of letters. ☐

Student can copy a word with accuracy. ☐

Student can copy a complete sentence with accuracy. ☐

Student is placing letters correctly within lines. ☐

Student can identify which movement group letters belong to (downstroke, closed anti-clockwise, open anti-clockwise, clockwise). ☐

Student can identify and colour wedges. ☐

Student can write numerals 1–100. ☐

Student can self-assess with accuracy. ☐

Notes:

....

....

Date: ....

CERTIFICATE

get.ga/PMWC150